What about her?

Thank you for your purchase of this book.

100% of the proceeds will be donated to different women's funds organizations. I don't want the money; I want a better environment.

Everything in this book was written by Ok Waleed
Copyright © 2021 OK WALEED.
All rights reserved.
Published by OK WALEED
ISBN: 9798576785797

A Very Short Preface

All the women who have come into and gone from my life have taught me how to be a better man and have helped me become the person I am today.

A woman is what raised me, sacrifice her body for my sake, and continue to teach me values I wouldn't have otherwise cared for.

The purpose of writing this book is to show appreciation for the opposite gender, to show my love, my hatred, my confusion with them but most of all what they mean to me. Although I am me, I couldn't have been that without them. Every wise and knowledgeable man knows this.

Men and women use each other, how else can we coexist.

Now I don't want to make this preface any longer cause we both know I hate a long preface so; Welcome, and thank you.

To:
     The women in my life, past, present, and future. To the ones who hate my guts, to the ones who just can't get enough of me, and of course the ones who forgot I existed. Thank you for continuing to add on to my character and who I will become. Even if your time feels as if it was wasted, I cherished every second of it.

At the touch of love, I became a poet.

As a man, you should be helping to work towards equality. Fight the sexism, patriarchy, psychical and sexual abuse. Be better for everyone around you.

I'm trying to right my wrongs but it's funny how my wrongs helped me write…

Acknowledgements:

The reader or whoever, I don't really care.

Contents:

Chapter 1: **Sorry**

Invisible Woman ……………………….………...…...13
I'm a feminist in another life ………………………....14
Share your location indefinitely…………………..…15
I love you Ramona flowers……………………………16
I called my sister a hoe……………………………..…17
Easier said than done………………………………….18
Gambling addiction…………………………………….19
Rolling in your sleep……………………………...……20
Lara Croft's Tomb…………………………….…..……21
22 with a life alert……………………………….….…22
Why did Coretta put up with it?..........................23
Musashi Miyamoto………………………………..……24
Making it about me again……………………….……25
Thief in the night………………………………….……26
Free Kill Bill……………………………………….……27
My bestie my bestie my best friend………………….28
HER……………………………………………….………29
Medusas' Eyes………………………………….………30
Baby Boy……………………………………….…..……31
Parasite……………………………………….…………32

Chapter 2: **There**

Ma you have horrible taste……………………....………35
I'M NOT YOUR BOYFRIEND!!!……………………36
Tony Soprano and his Psychiatrist……………………37
Destiny Ajaye ……………………………………………38
Adam took a bite too……………………………………39
Duce Bigalow: Male Gigolo…………………………….40
Tinder is for losers………………………………………42
Cat Calling……………………………………………….43
Mother Goose……………………………………………44
Picking up chicks at the library…………...……………45
The frustration being with a poet………………....……46
In prison while my girl hoeing…………………………47
I'll abandon you and my kids one day………………..48
Stanzas & Heartbreak…………………………………..49
I say I don't care but I-…………………………………50
Vegas Strippers………………………………………….51
I'm only going to say this once………………………..52
No WIFI No LTE No Connection……………………..53
Long lost member of Aventura…………………………54
I remember the first time I cheated…………….………55
Gang is love……………………………………………..56
Don't throw my shit out the window………………….57

Interlude:

Chapter 3: Is

    If my wife finds me overdosed…………………..................71
    You're a bozo……………………………….......................72
    Carlton Jr……………………………………….....…..........73
    Father Issues……………………………………..................74
    No Mask 2020……………………………………......….......75
    Dio's World……………………………………….................76
    Sorry we can't be friends……………………...…................77
    Wasted Times………………………………….....................78
    Karate Kid…………………………………………................79
    I can't afford her……………………………….....................80
    Rest in Peace Ruth George…………………….................81
    Think about it for a second……………………...................82
    Jennifer Lopez in Enough………………….......................83
    Birds of Prey……………………………………...................84
    Ginobli off the bench …………………………...…..............85
    Yeah, so what……………………………….........................86
    Why else would I live……………………….…....................87
    I'm such a sucker for irony……………………....................88
    Well irony and symbolism, they get me going…..................89
    And I love her..90

Interlude:

Chapter 4: No

As a woman..…..............93
Pussy and religion are all that matters.............................94
The females in my family...95
You tripping..96
Icveivrevqg8eqchfpqfu7fuiw...97
I really do hate women...98
Ok I don't really hate women I love them..................…..............99
The Male Rati..100
I was a C-section Procedure...101
Fuck I have writers' block!!!!!!!!!!!!!!!!!!!!........................102
Hijabi..103
Mary Jane...104
Zazie Beetz...105
Her voice...….......……....106
What a woman thinks...…......108
I hate when she moves on...109
My problem..…..........110

10

Chapter 5: Theme

Biorhythms..112
Don't defund Planned Parenthood....................113
Marion Crane..114
TW// Funny Quick Story................................116
Call me anytime 704-437-7285.......................117
Be honest..118
I find it romantic..119
Can we get paid maternity leave started..........120
Good morning text..121
2001: Space Odyssey....................................122
I saw your pictures together on Instagram........123

Interlude:

I know you want me to open up......................125
Heartbroken after I get caught cheating............126
My first crime towards a woman.....................127
Regret is greater than gratitude.......................128
Strippers make the best food..........................129
Alone again...130
When it was over..131

Outro:

About me:

11

Chapter 1: Sorry

Invisible Woman

losing my virginity

to someone
I didn't love

can't
even remember

her face
her name
her favorite color

she used me
as if it was her job
then clocked out

in the moment
I fell for it, of course
No self-control

looking back at it…

I wish…

I'm a feminist in another life

The disrespect
never an excuse for it

underrated, underappreciated
that theme keeps going

I write this as a hypocrite
from the outside
in

you deserve more
it should be about you
not to sound like a simp

there should be more than 31 days
to appreciate that history

       but whatever

just know
I care
 if it matters

Share your location indefinitely

trust issues
the serious problem
created by failed relationships

boyfriend girlfriend mom dad

but you have to…

    Ok this may sound crazy
    just hear me out

give that person
the benefit of the doubt

trust them
until they give you a reason

not to

I'm not saying be naive

but I am saying
have faith

I love you Ramona Flowers

she's the one I've been dreaming about
wishing I could feel her
be with her

she probably won't ever know how I feel
taking melatonin, taking xanax

so, I can see her more
minutes turn hours

I've known you forever
I don't know you at all

the only way
we can have more time

is if I fall asleep forever
                      will she still be there?

   …if it isn't guaranteed

then I guess I'll stay up

I called my sister a hoe

she ran away from home
just to see some boy

she's risking
getting kidnapped
getting killed

for the thrill

my mother has more patience
I don't

in her face
yelling

"Is being a whore what you want!?"
"you want to be a hoe out there for anybody!?"
"What the fuck is wrong with you!?"

I was wrong
she's going to be whoever she wants to be

can't control
can't dictate

she is who she is, that is okay
my love for her won't change

if you ever read this, I'm sorry, you aren't alone,
you can always come to me,

You can go home.

easier said than done

you aren't Beyoncé
so, what

Beyoncé
isn't you

the

bad shit you see in yourself
isn't true

acceptance

is what's needed
not from them
from you

is where we start

I hope you can understand
It's easier said than done

Gambling addiction

The unprotected sex
isn't scary

`cause I love you

If I die of disease
there's 2 lines on the test
I never see you again

it was worth it
`cause it was more than just

Rolling in your sleep

Sorry to women
who can relate to Adele
sigh, because of me

Lara Croft's Tomb

writing about the female body
no matter how much exploring
can't figure it out

understanding your secrets
seeing your flaws
feeling your shame

I see perfection

you see disproportions

…

I will never get it
so, I'll keep my mouth shut
but I will let you know

I appreciate the naturally created

22 with a life alert on my neck

a mistake
I fell for you
didn't hurt that much

came back to you
only to
hurt more

leaf in the wind
the way I enjoy
these falls

Why did Coretta put up with it?

I was with
    someone else

thoughts of you
    never left

thinking
    they could never be you

hurting you
    trying to find a temporary fix

for your permanent love
    I don't expect you to forgive me

    I could never forgive myself

Musashi Miyamoto

you aren't around

I try to find other women
To fill that loneliness

no excuse
all truth

I'm with them
It's still loneliness

                      (what a plot twist huh)

inside them
It's still there

they love me
loneliness continues to hold me

I remain seeing them
hoping that

They make me feel as complete
As you make me

This is my insanity

making it about me again

money
   power
      respect

desires of a man

what about the man who desires nothing?

Death is all to look forward to

he can see his friends and family
who have passed

   How selfish though

what about the friends and family
who haven't passed

I'm split apart

Thief in the Night

stole your innocence

robbed you blind with lies

telling you

"I'll stay"

took your jewels
cashed them out
paid for my ego

you will remember me forever
in that case

don't forgive me
learn from me

Free Kill Bill

To: Men

with

broken dreams
distraught hearts

Understand
women aren't here
to fix you

they can help

but it was never
their role
to fashion you

My bestie my bestie my best friend

talks to me
about the men who abuse her
use her

that don't appreciate her
when they do

they use her again

seeing someone you love
getting less
than what they deserve

it upsets me
knowing your worth

you should
get everything
you desire

HER

    Long distance relationships
    Aren't real

people between signals are

    secrets they share
    feelings they have
    touch that they long for

it's real

    reality hits
    you realize

    you're delusional
    it's not worth it

    you can't stop
    no other like her
    so, you continue, you continue, continue…

you're back where you started
    she doesn't exist

Medusas' Eyes

falling for any lady I see
beauty
intelligence

the two that'll
make me stay

the lust
will turn me to stone

the love
will make me feel alive again

Baby Boy

      I hate the women who tempt me
Leave me alone demons

although
I am just as wrong

Looking at my phone
Only reason it's continued
this long
texting you back

I am guilty
you were the snake

      Is the victim to temptation the one to blame?
      were they just too weak to resist?

Parasite

she tells me
she loves me
even when I abuse her
mentally, physically…

she clings to me
doesn't mind losing her life to me
I ask, why me
why me

she says
she loves me
then she says
do you love me
yes, I do
I do

falling to my knees...
she falls with me
laid down in pain...
she'll lie down with me
I'm wrong and I know I'm wrong...
she's willing to be right with me

I need her or love her...
I hate her too
she's better than me
I project
I call her names
I yell at her like she just doesn't matter
I abuse her as if…… it's me I see
I tell her lies
but she

continues
to sleep peacefully

or so it seems

she's turned over motionless
tears flow on the pillow

she wakes up the next day
a smile and breakfast

I question why
why does she continue
to love me?

I take out my insecurities on her as if
it was her! who placed them there

yet, she takes them
places them on her
she can bear it

I was never taught how to love
I only saw the arguments
step-pops and moms
fighting and yelling
they lay next to each other at the end

this is the love I would always see
as I grew older
it's not the love that has to be

It can be better
I can be better.

Chapter 2: There

Ma you have horrible taste

men
my mom was with

weren't good enough

not to be biased but my mother is
a perfect human being

today's world
that's priceless

yet,
the ones she's come across
treat her as if she's less
I fight for her, she holds me back

she stays with them
I don't know why

I hope
she knows
she's more than that

I just want you to get the happiness you deserve I just want you to find the love that I have found, the unconditional love you give your children I hope one day somebody else can show you that love… not because you need it but because you deserve to experience it forever. Although you've experienced that with God, I wouldn't be against the idea if you experienced it with another human.

IM NOT YOUR BOYFRIEND!!!

used each other
for one night
both consented to

    next day

you've called me 7 times
worried about where I'm going
your attached to me

    day after next at 11:43pm

    You up? happens

leave me on seen
we move on from each other

    The cycle repeats

Tony Soprano and his Psychiatrist

hopelessness
I feel

as if the world
doesn't matter

no one I can turn to
no one I can trust

she's always there

the woman
I place my burdens on
tears that I'm not scared to show

the world
our relationship

a one-way street
she knows this…

she is,
still willing to drive

Destiny Ajaye

the black woman
born with
two strikes
entering this world

black people are hated
women aren't respected

imagine this feeling
everybody vs you

even the ones
supposed to be with you,
against you

in reality everyone is afraid
of the potential

Power
Dedication
Love

you are a black woman
they will write you down in history
as hostile with warped dishonesties
Do not let them see you down

as another black woman said

"Still, I Rise"

Adam took a bite too

the first lady,
what let the world believe
that it was only you

Eve,
you are

No temptress
No seducer
No deceiver
No liar

You are not to blame
If anything, thank you

Another example of God's mercifulness

You both committed the sin
He forgave you both

That is the lesson
I took

Deuce Bigalow: Male Gigolo

      I bring her pleasure

thoughts pass

what will Egypt be like?
will I actually run for governor?
will I ever see this woman again?

I scramble, looking for my draws
She's in the bathroom redoing her hair
I stare at the bedroom mirror, naked reflection

What am I doing here?
Does she even know how to pronounce my name?
Who used who?

      now we are clothed

lying in bed laughing, smiling
whatever's on tv

patience runs thin
how do I get myself out of this?
text my friend? tell em call me?
or do I flat out say I'm leaving

The duality with this
I'm a good guy
who just happens to be dick?
no pun intended

      I don't want to be around her anymore

we used each other

That's all it was
That's all it could ever be

don't think too much of me
I'm not thinking of you

I love the plants in your house
and maybe that you trusted me

that's what bothering me
Why would you?

Not even a first date or coffee
your desires were so much

That you trusted me
It paid off of course

you got what you wanted
Now I'm the one feeling

shame
regret
pain

I've always admired women
when it's business
it's just business

Tinder is for losers

We swiped,
Right of course

We matched

Neither of us
Makes a move

So, we swipe again
Right of course

Cat Calling

I was never a fan of chasing women

As if I was Jack chasing Wendy through those halls

It seemed unnecessary to me

Because a conversation always went both ways

Fellas, please read the next words carefully.

She doesn't want to be bothered by you.

So out of respect, don't go out your way to bother her.

Mother Goose

It's almost hilarious
how we disrespect women

It's almost as if we forget
How we were brought in,

she decided not to abort you
she settled not to take the plan b
she realized how toxic her life was with him

So, she did what was right

All so you
disrespect women even more

Picking up chicks at the library

I walk in,
seemingly endless works of literature,
I notice her,
glasses, brown 4c hair, focused

I head to the non-fiction section
I hate the non-fiction section

hopefully she notices
my presence
she glances up
then goes back to her MacBook

I exist

So now what
"hey what you reading?"
Sigh, what if it's math homework

I should just leave her alone
I catch myself staring
in wonder or maybe amazement
Then she catches me

I look away, I walk out

next day
I walk in
superficially infinite creations

She notices me

The frustration being with a poet

it's not like
I talk in stanzas

Or say something philosophical
when you ask me "would you like toast"?

does it bother you
when I reveal secrets
secrets, you never known

the world knows now,
I wouldn't feel complete
without feeling vulnerable

no reason to be afraid
no matter what they read

they can never understand
I just hope
they understand themselves

In Prison while my girl hoeing

At that point.
when the judge's hammer slams

Sentenced

12 years

been with her for 3 years

tell me

will she wait
will she move on

or both

I'll abandon you and my kids one day

What will you do?

pick your head up and realize you never needed no m-

go out and find me?

Where would you start
you hate me for what I've done?
Who was I?
please wait for me
I'll be back for you and them
Will I ever be back?
I did this to you
Just go! find somebody new
Where can I find you when I return?
your first words to me
What will be your last?

Do what you have to

Stanzas & Heartbreak

what we had
is what you needed

It hurts you to
you see me in a hurry

the reason I don't kiss you
I got someone

I actually make love with her
I have respect for her

So I disrespect you
you mean more to someone else

I say I don't care but I-

She'll remember me
for the rest of her life

trying to find another me
in him

there isn't
continue to put on that mask

put your time and feelings
into someone who isn't me

I need you to try
not for me

I want happiness for you

Vegas strippers

aroma of sin
I bask in it

Take me to the back
you're doing this for college

give me your number
I don't save it

you made me feel loved
in the moment

even though
none of it is real

it almost seems as if
everything is real

you show yourself
and hide

I don't blame you,
we all hide who we are

I'm only going to say this once

Stop watching porn

not real
not healthy
not what you need

I'm a fan of moderation
When it comes to anything

When it comes to this
I can't tolerate it

Do not continue to support
an industry that exploits women.

Try chewing 5 gum or something

No WIFI No LTE No Connection

we use to talk everyday
now nothing
we're strangers again

we can't be friends
that's just not possible
not after we loved each other

I wish we didn't split apart
Now all my texts are green
time worked against us

you forget the good times
quick to remember why you hate me

I love it

Long lost member of Aventura

Dime mi amor
te arrepientes
estar con un hombre como yo
yo era lo que llamaste seguro
ahora la única cosa que te mantuvo así
te ha lastimado
sin embargo tu vuelves a mi siempre vuelves a mi siempre
no te amo
ahora eres libre

pero tu sabes
nuestro amor es más que palabras
no es tan fácil dejarlo ir

conmigo eres feliz
conmigo estas triste

I remember the first time I cheated

I promise, it wasn't planned
It just…. happened

when you told me, you found out
didn't answer my calls
wouldn't text me

anger
hurt
It wasn't your fault

The girl wasn't you

sun was going down
It was windy out
I was hungry
friends were there

Everything on my mind
besides her

Yet, it happened
She kissed me (on camera smh)
I didn't kiss her back
But I did
So, I lied too

I can't imagine how many times you watched the video
we were kids but even then, I knew
what was right from wrong
I was wrong

I'm Sorry

Gang is Love

a scary part of my life is that
I'm willing to throw it away
for you

If something happened to you
I would turn the city
upside down

it's more than just loyalty with you
when you make out
the trenches

I'm willing
to go right back
with you

Because shit if we made it out once
We should get
lucky again…

That's the type of mindset
that made me lose it all
in the first place

Don't throw my shit out the window

the reason
for this poly lifestyle
not enough love
for myself

I find as many women
that will love me

don't have to accept me
if you do, thank you

I've been trying hard

to accept myself

Interlude:

Thank you for reading the first two chapters, can we get a round of applause for the ladies out there tonight? *crowd applause*

When I was about 13 years old, my big homie was explaining to my other friends why I'm not like them. As I try to remember, he said something along the lines of. (sorry if I misquote you J.O)

"He ain't like the rest of yall, he's not just tryna fuck bitches and get hoes. He actually wants a relationship and love and all that shit it come with"

You were wrong and you were right.

I remember him saying that because I thought "Damn is it really 'cause I'm light skin that I have these feelings or is it really because I actually desire love.?" Who knows? I just know as I grew up, I've spoken to a lot of different women romantically, sexually, and platonically. I've grown to have an appreciation for the women that entered my life and decided they just wanted to break my heart. I also appreciate the ones whose hearts I've had to break, no hard feelings anymore, I hope.

The hidden chapter are just women who come across my mind once in a while, mainly because I've actually learned something from them. What not to do, what to do better and what I should do instead. Shout out to you for making me the man I am today, but it's a skeleton I could never dig up again.

Hidden Chapter: Graveyard

———

you ever get this book
Go read page 55 again.

we moved past it,
we cool now.

my guilt dies with me

You used me

to get back at my brother

I'm happy
our blood's
thicker than water

I was a pawn
for your revenge

it showed me
never to break a code

No matter
the temptation

It's not worth
a bond

It's not worth
losing a friend

Sorry you guys didn't work out

Deep down

                        I know

you deserved better
than me

than how I
treated you

I wanted to congratulate you
I knew my place

I'm happy for you
you're living better

———

you're actually crazy

mad scientist

I should have taken you seriously

then again,
we both knew

                                                            it was a joke

from the start

thanks
for teaching
what I needed

Even after
it's all said
seems done
you stick by me
calling me once every year
to check up
or maybe make me check on you

you obviously haven't given up.

Give up.

———

should have never
met my mom

after that

I wanted to play "dad"
a kid that wasn't mine

shows
how much you meant

I learned
to be straight forward

Not lead them on
get their hopes up

Thanks.

My first love
The sweetest love
Eventually the most toxic love

                                        Hope everything is ok

first
to break my heart

first
to cheat on me

In that order

It was meant for me
I don't blame you

I was distant
He was local

Call me Neo
The way I dodged the bullet

———

I couldn't give you
what you wanted

at the time
I didn't know

it wasn't right
leading you on

As If you were only useful to me
When it hit 11:43pm

You are more

You are more than

I could
appreciate

———

we never met
you love me

as if we did

you also
hate me

as if we did

what technology
has done for us

what little
humans need

to feel
emotions

I find it… interesting

Chapter 3: Is

If my wife finds me overdosed

I had happiness
                              don't worry
Pray
I'm in a better life

it wasn't intentional

I feel bad
                              about
the fact
you'll have to see me like that

Cold
Lifeless
Emotionless

                              Me

I'm sorry
you had to see me like that
most of the time.

You're a Bozo

I can tell you every human
is created equally

since you aren't with me
you know it's a lie now

be serious for one second.

Are you serious?

How could you downgrade like that?

everything I showed you
taught you

How you do yourself like that

Oh well,

More power to you baby.

Carlton Jr.

    momma cried when I told her
        I got a white girl

    she knows the evil

    for my first
she's pure
        I kept her forever

    a woman that accepts me
    was worth

    a thousand bitches
    that just wanted me

    crazy
    my momma always saying now

    "You got a good girl, treat her right"

    I've known

Father issues

another girl

with no father figure
in her life

just another girl

that will make
my life easier

No mask 2020

Bare face

right when you're done crying
I comfort you

I wasn't the one
that hurt you

                You're crying about school

Isn't it funny?
perturbing

about one day

For that
one day

But I'll be that
one person

For
your lifetime

Dio's World

Every woman I ever talked to

I wanted the best

for them

The best wasn't me

it was just the best they could do

at the time

that's ok

Sorry we can't be friends

I hate pretty women
I love them as well

Falling for the beauty
Before I fall for her

Who would she be to me?
If I was blind

Wasted Times

once again
you regret
your decisions

he lied
you thought things
would be different

Karate Kid

as I chase you
skeletons chase me

realizing loving you
means more

I ignore you
you're still there

waiting to love me
till I'm ready

I can't afford her

she takes a picture of her lobster

      The flash wasn't on
      hold on

she takes a picture of her lobster

puts it on Instagram

women I will never
be with

I can't afford her
I can accept that

she wants

stars on the roof
courtside seats
personal chef

she'll never see

she's a star to me
but no matter how much I ball out
it won't be enough to fill her up

there's always going to be better

I don't trip I get better

Rest in Peace Ruth George

women have it bad in this world

as men we make it harder

   imagine the fear of "what will he do if I say no"

so, she gives him a fake phone number in hopes

that'll satisfy his thirst

We should protect our women and continue to educate our men. In the end, evil will continue to exist so at that point, ladies protect yourself and gentlemen educate your brothers. We can't destroy evil but we can continue to beat it up so it doesn't beat us down. This takes good from all sides. Anything can happen to anybody, I just want you to be prepared, I want you to be safe. We can't be liberated without the liberation of our women.

Think about it for a second

you know, a freed slave
was able to vote before
any woman could

Jennifer Lopez in Enough

I apologize

that you go through this
evil he places on you

> I want to tell you
> match that evil
>
> Be stronger,
> show him the feeling
>
> Fear. Despair. Hate.

"Two wrongs don't make a right"
I get that,

sometimes you need to do wrong
So, you can get yourself right

Birds of Prey

To all the women
In my group therapy,

I can take your trauma
Take your pain

Just to see you live a happy life
there isn't any hope for me

I have hope for you

You are not defined by what broke you.

Ginobli off the bench

the sidelines
it's cool, it's whatever
don't have to deal with pressure
performing
taking big shots

on sidelines
wait for your number
run around for a few minutes
then let the starter back in

I guess… it can be ok…

Until I want to start
I want to know the feelings

hitting a game winner
playing more minutes

if you're on the bench
the spot
can always be replaced

Then you aren't playing anymore.

Yeah, so what

telling you, that I
love you, adore you, `cause it's
convenient for me

Why else would I live?

keeping a gun, so
then whenever she leaves me
I can also leave

I'm such a sucker for irony,

I hope

a female

kills me

well Irony and symbolism, they get me going.

    If I pick my death
assisted suicide

    Line up
    all the women I've loved

    9mm guns
    hollow points, of course

    let them shoot

                      they killed me once

                        shouldn't be hard

                        a second time

And I love her

she gives me nothing
worthy of a diamond

a knife my lover brings
she puts into me

and I love her

dark as the cave that dulls
deep as the sky

this love of mine
will most likely die

…. And I love her….

Interlude:

So, let me take a short break from all this boring poetry and show you what the words my mentor/professor *Andrew Payne* had told me on happiness.

"The answer to finding happiness: breaking with the mad simulation of everyday life—the media drummed-up nonsense, the marketing schemes conditioning us to see happiness as being a certain way, the political ideals that tell us our happiness is contingent on giving politicians power over us, etc.—and living for one's own sake, taking joy in that which is real: friendship, the experience of nature, and the deeper heart of human creativity."

I guess I'm doomed huh? But less about me I hope you take this and remind yourself how to obtain the happiness you seek. Oh, and if you already have that happiness daily. ~~Fuck You.~~

Just kidding, I envy you. So please don't take your blessings for granted because it can be stripped faster than you got them.

Chapter 4: No

As a woman

You are not defined by your sex appeal

You are not defined by your breasts

You are not defined by your mood

You are not defined by your vagina

You are not defined by your decisions

You are not defined by your mistakes

You are not defined by your thoughts

don't care if you knew this already
I just wanted to remind you.

Pussy and religion are all that matters

my mind, filled with regrets and endless bouts
while I was in the east, trying her figure out
God had plans, better than any route

I always took them for granted
a seed, was all what she wanted
in my loneliest time, God was planted

in my most vulnerable moment, I cried to her
what a fool I was, I was played like an amateur
while I was lost and naïve, He became my chauffeur

as I spent time away from it, by myself
I wrote a book wanting you, to look at yourself
I apologize, I astray away... I thought of only self

then I spent more time, with that woman
encouraged me to be a slave of god, the best man
although I may iniquity, I never lost His plan

The females in my family

my mother who taught me
Love and Forgiveness

my sister who taught me
Patience and Protecting

my grandma who taught me
Wisdom and Caretaking

my aunt who taught me
Drinking and Enjoyment

You Tripping

    been talking for 4 months
        unprotected sex

    I met your family
        heard of mine

    we talk
        Every. Single. Day.

    you know my hopes and dreams
        I know yours

    that doesn't mean
        get your hopes up

    I'm still single

Icveivrevqg8eqchfpqfu7fuiw

I have writers' block so…

I think of you…you…you…you
of course, you…and you

muses for this art
same poetry I hate

when I write about you
rolls right off of my fingers

I love it

If you never existed

would I even have
anything to write about

I really do hate women

      annoyance I get

blowing up my phone
questioning where I was
asking for this, for that

      I just want to leave you

      then I remember

      the good in you

      I remember

the love I get

Ok I don't really hate women I love them!

pole to pay for college
camera to pay rent
body to post with

    end of the day
    it doesn't matter

    a bitch, a hoe, a lady.

    In the end
    doesn't matter

    continue doing what you're doing

    ah
    I am a feminist

    You see the way I encourage women

    I just want the best for you
    Less stress for you
    It creates a better you

The Male Rati

I don't love myself

I seek out women
That will love me

As many women as I can

To help this ventricular septal defect
As many women it takes

To feel a reason, they love me

Maybe

I was a C-Section procedure

    didn't cry when I was born

    The doctor slapped my ass
    made it happen

I was the most comfortable in my life

    All these poems about momdukes
    Got me looking like a momma's boy

    But in all seriousness

    That's where I find my comfort
    In a woman's arms

    she can barely lift my big head

    The effort
    The security

Fuck I have writers' block!!!!!!!!!!!!!!!!!

AHHHHHHHHHHHHHHHHHHHHHHHHHHHHH
HHHHHHHHHHHHHHHHHHHHHHHHHHHHHH
HHHHHHHHHHHHHHHHHHHHHHHHHHHHHH
HHHHHHHHHHHHHHHHHHHHHHHHHHHHHH
HHHHHHHHHHHHHHHHHHHHHHHHHHHHHH
HHHHHHHHHHHHHHHHHHHHHHHHHHHHHH
HHHHHHHHHHHHHHHHHHHHHHHHHHHHHH
HHHHHHHHHHHHHHHHHHHHHHHHHHHHHH
HHHHHHHHHHHHHHHHHHHHHHHHHHHHHH
HHHHHHHHHHHHHHHHHHHHHHHHHHHHHH
HHHHHHHHHHHHHHHHHHHHHHHHHHHHHH
HHHHHHHHHHHHHHHHHHHHHHHHHHHHHH
HHHHHHHHHHHHHHHHHHHHHHHHHHHHHH
HHHHHHHHHHHHHHHHHHHHHHHHHHHHHH
HHHHHHHHHHHHHHHHHHHHHHHHHHHHHH
HHHHHHHHHHHHHHHHHHHHHHHHHHHHHH
HHHHHHHHHHHHHHHHHHHHHHHHHHHHHH
HHHHHHHHHHHHHHHHHHHHHHHHHHHHHH
HHHHHHHHHHHHHHHHHHHHHHHHHHHHHH
HHHHHHHHHHHHHHHHHHHHHHHHHHHHHH
HHHH

Hijabi

You have my utmost respect

    The difficulty

    I can't even imagine

    The stride

    for piety

    is one I wilted with

if you find yourself
    getting disrespected

                           remember

you have more support
    than any evil eyes

    can equivalate too

Mary Jane

the one
who's always there

ready

for my problems
taking them away

for this moment
I love you

it comes with a price
always worth it

in the moment

losing it all for you
losing myself for you
losing my mind for you

I don't mind

Zazie Beetz

imagining my life, with a stranger
disregarding what I have now
leaving everything

brought you flowers
Tulips
I don't know if you liked them
your favorite color is wine red
you don't drink wine though
sorry, obviously no correlation

I see us together
because we aren't together
does that make sense?
I want something to happen so bad…
I imagine it for my comfort

you smile when we talk
don't be afraid if I won't accept you

you're everything I want
+ more

Until I'm
I'm bored of you
we fall out like
we never met before

that's what hurts the most
in my mind
we've lived
three times before

Her Voice

    gets me out of bed
    makes me want to do something
    (other than show her how pathetic I am)

    she's motivation
    she isn't trying to be
    just tells me about her day
look at my day
I want to have a better one
something I can tell her about

    just another bum
I am
    contemplate suicide
I do
    drugs every chance I get
I try

    so, I lie to her
    make myself seem productive
get out of bed
    hear the happiness in my voice
making up for pain
    pain I'll never show

woke up at 6am this morning
stayed in bed till 3pm

    Time flies
    When you're thinking of time

    30 minutes go by
    She has to go *ends call*

Now what…

I progress to who I was
no, I can't
    mint on my breath
    fed the cat
    checked the mail
    read the news
    made plans for this party

All in 30 mins just because of you

now that you're not here

back to bed

sleep, and then wake up, then sleep again
stare at the ceiling and imagine a better life

  I want to do all the things
  I know you wouldn't stand for

  sorry I lied to you

  I was hiding the person I am

  so, you can have the person I thought you wanted

What a woman thinks

    You don't understand

    The self-consciousness

hides it so well
    you wouldn't know
    even if you inspected her

    when the time comes and
    she reveals it

embrace it

    It will feel like a mistake for her
    but you need to show her

    Show her
    Teach her

    that's just not the case

I hate when she moves on

fuck you
for being happy

finding yourself
with somebody else

yall corny and lame

-

I miss you
still love you
trying to rekindle a flame

even though
we gain nothing from it

Fuck you
I don't need you
You need me
I know you do
I made you

Whatever

My problem

      a real reason to live
      can't really think of one

        outside of family and God

I talk to her
    I have more time left

when we aren't talking

      hopeless
      depressed
      high again

Can I be any more pathetic?

Chapter 5: Theme

Biorhythms

Her heart
    An acre with room to grow

    It breaks…time and time again
    still continues to beat

    Hope that there is more
    the sun will be up

Her heart stops,
    doesn't wake up again
    still
    impression has been left
    she meant something

although her heart stopped

    memories
    anger
    love

it continues

she is more than just her body

Don't defund Planned Parenthood

Coming from a
low-income community

there needs to be more places
that give resources when it comes to sex
protection of silent killers
    as a man
a woman's choice regarding abortion doesn't pertain to me

but my choice to get sexually educated
having the tools to be ready and protected

can prevent a woman
from making that difficult choice

    this isn't political it's people we're talking about.

Marion Crane

faking the same interest
rehearsing the same lines

    we meet
    I get what I want

    the experience
always a different
      look in her eyes
      happiness in her voice
      smile she wants to hide

    I enjoy every second
    dinner
    lunch

    I am important
    don't get me wrong
    it's not for personal ego

    I have to gain something
    after the bill,
    after time spent

    even if that something is

    "Thank you for taking me out"
    Then I proceed with
    "yeah, I enjoyed it I hope to see you again"

It's funny
I never want to see her again

don't want anything to do with her
don't respond to her texts
mute her on twitter

I had a great time.
I want to see her again.
I will regret this.

But...

I want to be missed
blowing up my phone
putting her pride aside for me

she realized
she hasn't met someone like me
she won't lose me

how many women
have I done this to

take their breath away

Then move on
the eupnea bandit

not you
me

TW// Funny Quick Story

    I was sexually assaulted as a kid
by my cousin

        she was

        older
        family

                      trust came easy

        I don't think of it
        I dreamt it
no,
        it was real
        it was wrong

        should have
        said something…anything
        I was a kid….

                      who could I trust,

        it's been years now

        haven't spoke to her
        never will expose her

        She has a good life
        I want her to be happy

call me anytime 1-704-437-7285

You will always belong to me

part of your heart
deep in your memories
once in a while in your thoughts

You will always belong to me

on your third kid with him
you're getting married but didn't invite me
you decide you're done with me

You will always belong to me

when I'm finally happy
I accomplish everything,
even when I am dead

Sorry for brainwashing you

Be honest

Do you hate me?
Because you loved me

it makes you happy
seeing me unhappy

I hate you
Just as much

I'm sorry for always asking questions

I find it romantic

The prophet *SAW*

Died on a woman's lap

Now that I think about it

That might be the way to go

Can we get paid maternity leave started

calls you a bitch

you're faithful and respectful

calls you a lady

you feel like a city girl

calls you a female

you're more than that

what matters is how you feel,
responsibility you take for yourself

I hate that the real things always sound so corny

Good morning text

grandma texts me a prayer every morning
2 paragraphs

copies and pastes to me
I don't mind
at least she thought of me

I don't respond,
I don't say thanks,
Good morning,
Hey,
Or even a thumbs up reaction,

a week goes by
14 paragraphs to read

I miss her now
I guess I'll text her that

2001: Space Odyssey

    I went to a vegan restaurant by myself

waitress was attractive
checking on me every 7 minutes
I was there for 30 minutes
asked her four questions
       as I eat fake chicken nuggets
her curiosity in me spiked
only black person in this restaurant
she knew this wasn't my thing
nonetheless
she was absorbed in me
just wasn't trying to pay the bills
she wanted to know who I am
       the bill is here
cleaned up after myself
sip last bit of water
feel bad I didn't drink it all
drag myself to the cash register
       The food was terrible
she greets me with a smile
"I hope you enjoyed your meal"
       does anybody enjoy vegan food?
anyways,
"yeah, I did thanks"
"scribble right here for me"
       I leave a ten-dollar tip
the only number
she cared about anyways
I asked her one more question
nod my head in agreement
"Thanks, have a good day"

I saw your pictures together on Instagram

it bothers me
you threw all my lessons away

taught you to be better and do better

yet you settled for less
we aren't together,
but I know your worth

I want to dm you on the side
Can I get you back?

Testing your love

Those type of games
what broke us apart

we both love to play though

your mother misses me
that's enough

I hope he keeps you at the bare minimum satisfied...

Interlude:

I knew this book was going to be the hardest thing I will ever write. I really did try my best, I think. I struggled a lot though without making the writing seem cliché or cringy, at the end I wrote my thoughts, feelings, and truth, 'cause of that I was able to pull it off.

    I decided to call my mom and ask her if she had any advice when it came to writing about women. This what she had to say:

"Love and appreciate women. We are overlooked. We do more than you men. What we go through in life in general we have more balls. You can't feel pain as we feel pain just by bringing a child into the world. We work hard too; we work in the house we work outside we work all the time. I can keep going, if you want me to keep going. Really and truly, we need to be appreciated for everything we do. I think men overlook women because they think they're more superior. They should be kissing the floor we walk on."

Ma if you read this book, I'm sorry If you hate it.
Or I'm glad you like it!

I know you want me to open up

      trusted me
how could you

      I hate myself
you opened up and let me in
      is why I can never trust you
obviously, no good character judgement

it's not you
I don't like to be vulnerable
I'm paranoid

Fuck
Idk
Uhhh

It's you
your fault

I will continue to push you away
eventually you give
everyone gives up

I'm going to Little Darlings

Heartbroken after I get caught cheating

damn why couldn't you
mind your business

that,
that's temporary

me, you,
a forever thing

are you really going to let one time
or 394329560 times

Ruin what we have? house, cars, kids?

you really crazy
fuck it, I can't deal with you
I'm leaving
let me know
when YOU straighten yourself out

Please don't let me come back.

My first crime towards a woman

    my aunt

recently she went through a miscarriage

    As a kid
    I knew better

"that's why your baby dead"

    didn't realize it at first
    I broke her heart

    She chased me around to catch me
    To beat my ass

                            It probably happened

    Then she told my mom
    got my ass beat again

    what's worse
    it still bothers me

    I've apologized for it
    it still bothers me

    Why did I say that?
    Why did I want to hurt my family?

    Am I evil

Regret is greater than gratitude

maybe I miss you
because deep down I know that,
I was the problem

Strippers make the best food

my favorite women

Raw
Authentic
Fake
Dominate
Slimy
Submissive

whatever you need

everything

besides themselves

Alone again

When I'm by myself
The feeling is almost perfect

Perfection would be death

only way I can be myself
feeling of comfort

by myself
me and my thoughts

feels like my worst enemy
my most truthful one

feeling of loneliness can tear us apart
same reason we long for someone to pull us together

with you I still feel alone
I haven't spent time alone

I don't know what it's like to be by myself
What is that feeling…

When it was over

I was trying to find everything
That could replace you

I resorted to the drugs...
They were only real as they came

I thought more money
Thus, led to an endless path

I laid up with so many hoes
Trying to find you

I realized I couldn't find you
I found better instead

Outro:

So, the thing about being a poet, well for me at least.

"Poets treat their experiences shamelessly: they exploit them"

A quote from one of my favorite philosophers.

Everything I've written has been because of a first-hand or second-hand experience. The reason I exploit it isn't for money or fame but for others to barefacedly experience how I felt. I want you to be uncomfortable, I want you to be upset, I want you to enjoy it, I kind of don't want you to be depressed, 'cause that's the one thing I cannot beat…yet.

The hope of course, still alive.

I do enjoy writing; this is why I have lied to you all about not making a sequel. In reality, I am creating a trilogy. This book *'What about her?'* is only the second instalment, if you have it, I want to say thank you. We all know sequels usually SUCK. Yet, you decided to give my writing a chance, and yes sorry there was no art this time. I didn't get paid for the first book so management told me we had to make some budget cuts so sorry if the ink and paper isn't the best quality either. The trilogy will end once I have my first born, until then I will try to write everyday and over the years the collection will come together for the final book.

Thank you once again to my 15 fans out there. I see you! For completing this, my gift to you is a preview, the third and final book of the trilogy will be titled "Is this it?"

About me:

Read my autobiography *Who Are You?* By Ok Waleed

Made in the USA
Monee, IL
29 January 2023